Peter's Pets

Daisy Ross

INFOMAX COMMON CORE READERS

Rosen Classroom™

New York

Published in 2013 by The Rosen Publishing Group, Inc.
29 East 21st Street, New York, NY 10010

Book Design: Michael Harmon

Photo Credits: Cover einstein/Shutterstock.com; p. 5 © iStockphoto.com/JoyceMarrero; p. 7 Komar/Shutterstock.com; p. 9 shellyagami-photoar/Shutterstock.com; p. 11 anyaivanova/Shutterstock.com; p. 13 Jill Lang/Shutterstock.com; p. 15 Jeffery Hamilton/Lifesize/Getty Images.

ISBN: 978-1-4488-8929-7
6-pack ISBN: 978-1-4488-8930-3

Manufactured in the United States of America

CPSIA Compliance Information: Batch #WS12RC: For further information contact Rosen Publishing, New York, New York at 1-800-237-9932.

Word Count: 38

Contents

Peter throws a ball
to his dog.

Peter feeds his rabbit
a carrot.

Peter gives his cat
some water.

Peter gives his bird
a new toy.

Peter takes
his turtle outside.

Peter gives his crab
a new shell.

Words to Know

crab

rabbit

shell

turtle

Index